POLAR
ANIMALS

written by D Harper
illustrated by S Boni *and* L R Galante

Ladybird

CONTENTS

page

Where are the Poles? 5

The Arctic 6

The Antarctic 7

Ice all Around 8

Life in the Cold 10

Seals 12

Whales 14

Polar Bears 16

Walruses 17

Penguins 18

Birds 20

Life below the Ice 22

Exploring the Poles 24

People of the Poles 26

Amazing Polar Facts 28

Glossary 29

Index 30

WHERE ARE THE POLES?

The north and south poles lie at the very ends of the Earth. They are the coldest, windiest, most icy places on our planet. The **North Pole** is in the middle of the frozen Arctic Ocean. The **South Pole** is at the centre of the huge, ice-covered continent of Antarctica.

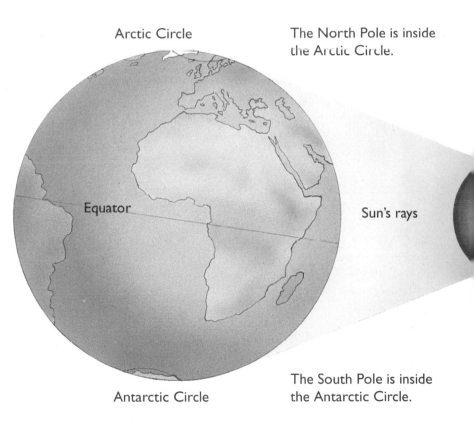

Arctic Circle

The North Pole is inside the Arctic Circle.

Equator

Sun's rays

Antarctic Circle

The South Pole is inside the Antarctic Circle.

The Sun's rays are strongest at the Equator, which is the broadest part of the Earth. The rays are weakest at the poles because the Earth is curved. This means that the poles are always colder than the rest of the Earth.

THE ARCTIC

The landscape in the Arctic is bleak because there is ice everywhere. No trees grow because it is too cold. The North Pole is an important geographical point. It lies on the nought degree line of longitude, an imaginary line that encircles the Earth.

The Arctic Circle

Here there is an area of land called **tundra** where most of the Arctic animals are found.

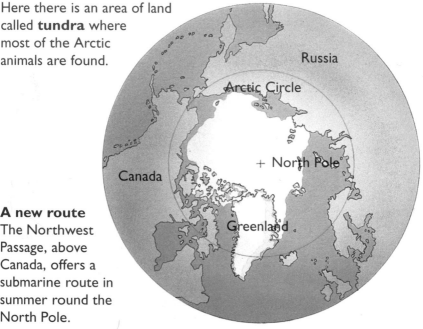

A new route

The Northwest Passage, above Canada, offers a submarine route in summer round the North Pole.

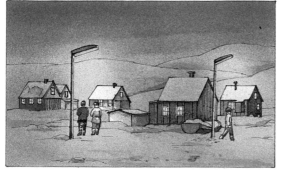

Perpetual darkness

In polar lands, during winter, the Sun never rises. It is dark for months. When it is winter in the Arctic, then it is summer in the Antarctic.

THE ANTARCTIC

The nought degree line of longitude runs round the Earth from the North Pole through to the South Pole. Antarctica is the fifth largest of the world's continents, but it is the only one where there are no local people. It is thought that no one had ever walked here until 1895.

The coldest place on Earth

Temperatures at the South Pole fall as low as -80°C. In spite of this, a number of scientists live and work here.

South America

Antarctic Circle

Ronne Ice Shelf

+ South Pole

Ross Ice Shelf

A remote place

Antarctica is separated from the rest of the world by more than 1,000 kilometres of rough, dangerous seas.

The midnight Sun

During the polar summer, the Sun never sets — it always shines even at midnight. When it is summer in the Antarctic, then it is winter in the Arctic.

ICE ALL AROUND

There is ice everywhere at the poles, as far as the eye can see. In the Arctic, an ice sheet covers most of the island of Greenland. Here the Quarayaq Glacier moves at a speed of up to twenty metres per hour every day. It is the fastest flowing glacier in the world.

① Growlers
These are small icebergs that have broken off from a big iceberg or the end of a glacier.

② Tabular icebergs
These are huge and are characterised by flat tops and sides.

③ Glaciers
Over thousands of years rivers of ice flow very slowly down a mountain or an ice cap, forming a glacier. Many glaciers eventually reach the sea.

The ice sheet covering the continent of Antarctica is up to four kilometres thick and millions of years old. It contains 90 per cent of all the ice on Earth, and it never melts. If it did, the sea level round the world would rise by up to one hundred metres, causing gigantic floods.

(4) Crevasses
Crevasses are deep cracks in the ice that are formed as a glacier moves along.

(5) Bergy bits
Bergy bits are chunks of ice that have broken away from large icebergs.

(6) Icebergs
Icebergs are gigantic chunks of ice that have broken off from an ice shelf or the end of a glacier. Only about one-eighth of an iceberg shows above the water.

LIFE IN THE COLD

Despite the bitter cold, howling winds and blizzards, an amazing number of animals live round the north and south poles. Some live on the ice itself, whilst others live in the freezing seas. All polar animals have adapted to the harsh weather conditions and have special features that help them survive in the cold.

Penguins
All types of penguin have a thick covering of water-resistant feathers. This stops the penguins becoming too cold or wet.

Arctic foxes
To lower the risk of attack, Arctic foxes change the colour of their fur in winter and summer to blend in with the background.

Snowshoe hares
Huge, wide feet stop snowshoe hares from sinking into soft snow.

Birds

Polar winters are too cold for most birds and so they fly to warmer climates for winter.

Seals

Seals have thick layers of fat, called blubber, under their skin. This helps to keep them warm.

Polar bears

Dense, waterproof coats keep the bears warm and dry.

SEALS

Seals live in both the Arctic and the Antarctic. They spend most of their time swimming and diving for fish and other seafood. Seals are well equipped for swimming – they have strong flippers, and their sleek, streamlined bodies cut through the water easily.

Diving for food
Although they are **mammals** and breathe air, seals can hold their breath for long periods as they dive underwater for food.

Arctic seals

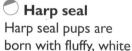 **Harp seal**
Harp seal pups are born with fluffy, white fur that darkens as the seal grows older.

Hooded seal
The 'bag' on the nose of the male swells when the seal becomes excited.

Ringed seal
The smallest of the polar seals, the ringed seal is only about one metre long.

◯ Southern elephant seal

This giant is the largest of all seals and can weigh up to 4,000 kilograms – as much as a small truck – and can be up to six metres long.

Antarctic seals

◯ Leopard seal

The leopard seal is a fierce hunter and uses its sharp teeth to catch penguins.

◯ Weddell seal

The Weddell seal uses its teeth to gnaw **breathing holes** in the ice.

◯ Crabeater seal

Despite its name, this seal mainly eats **krill**, sieving them through its teeth.

WHALES

Some of the largest creatures on Earth live in the icy Arctic and Antarctic seas. They include the huge blue whale, the biggest animal that has ever lived. Some whales live near the poles all year round, while others only come to the poles to feed in the summer.

Sperm whale
Like all whales, a sperm whale breathes through a **blowhole** on top of its head. When feeding, it dives to great depths in search of squid.

Narwhal
The long, spiralling **tusk** on the male narwhal is actually a tooth, which may be used for fencing with other males.

Blue whale
This huge animal eats tiny shrimp-like creatures, called krill. It strains them from the water, using its **baleen plates** as a sieve.

Killer whale
Swimming in packs, this hunter looks for groups of penguins, seals or fish. It also tips up ice floes to reach the seals resting on top.

Beluga whale
The newborn beluga is brown and then turns grey as it grows up. Once it reaches adulthood its skin is pure white.

POLAR BEARS

Polar bears live in the Arctic all year round, roaming along the coasts or floating out to sea on ice floes. Polar bears are twice as big as tigers and are powerful hunters. They eat mainly seals. A bear will wait by a seal's breathing hole until it comes up for air. Then the bear pounces, killing the seal with a single blow using its powerful paw.

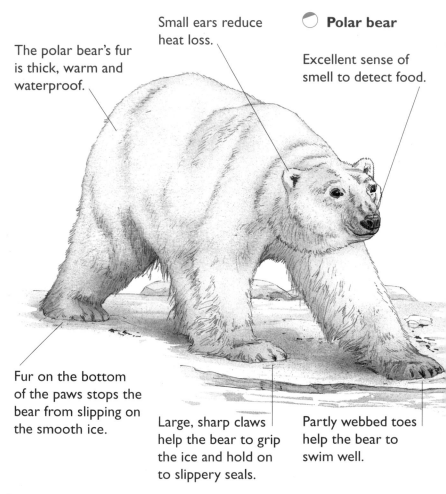

Small ears reduce heat loss.

Polar bear

The polar bear's fur is thick, warm and waterproof.

Excellent sense of smell to detect food.

Fur on the bottom of the paws stops the bear from slipping on the smooth ice.

Large, sharp claws help the bear to grip the ice and hold on to slippery seals.

Partly webbed toes help the bear to swim well.

SAVING THE POLES

The poles are fragile areas, and need to be protected for the future. The poles are among the last unspoilt places on Earth, and home to some of the world's rarest animals. They are also rich in resources such as fish, oil and valuable metals.

In the past, millions of whales, seals and penguins were killed for their meat, skins and other products. Several types of whales were almost hunted to extinction. Today, most countries have banned whaling.

The poles are being spoilt by rubbish left behind by scientists and tourists. Environmentalists would like to clean up the litter which is ugly, and dangerous to the polar wildlife.

Oil spills from tankers are a threat to wildlife. Scientists are worried that the Antarctic will be spoilt by exploration for oil and minerals. Scientists would like the Antarctic to be a protected World Park.

ANIMALS OF THE POLES

Southern elephant seal

Caribou

Polar bear

Weddell seal

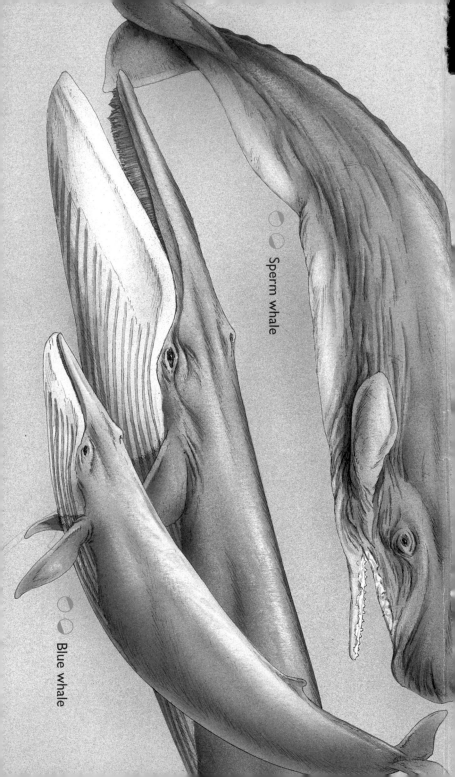

Sperm whale

Blue whale

Penguin

Walrus

Killer whale

Narwhal

Beluga whale

SURVIVING ABOVE AND BELOW THE ICE

Penguin

Gannet

Arctic tern

Little auk

Walrus

Puffin

Albatross

Arctic fox

WALRUSES

Walruses live in large **colonies** along the coasts of the Arctic Ocean. They hunt for food on the seabed, using their bristly moustaches to feel for clams, crabs and sea urchins. Walruses root food out with their tusks and snouts. Their tusks can grow longer than your arm. On land, walruses bask in the Sun to warm themselves.

The walrus uses its tusks, which are long teeth, for self-defence and for making air holes in the ice.

A walrus has very small eyes because the polar waters are too murky to see clearly and so it doesn't need large eyes.

Pinky-brown skin turns deeper pink as the walrus sunbathes.

○ **Walrus**

Walruses sometimes sleep in the water, hooking themselves onto the ice with their tusks. Large males can grow over four metres long and weigh up to 1,800 kilograms.

PENGUINS

There are no penguins in the Arctic, but several different types can be found in Antarctica. Although penguins cannot fly and they may look clumsy on land, their sleek bodies, partly webbed feet and flipper-like wings make penguins fast, graceful swimmers.

The Emperor
After the female lays the egg, the male looks after the egg until it hatches. Standing in the cold and wind for two months in the winter, the male emperor penguin eats nothing and hardly moves. He balances the egg on his feet with a flap of furry skin.

Speedy divers
Penguins can swim really fast and shoot out of the sea onto rocks.

The Adelie
One of the few birds native to Antarctica.

The Gentoo
The gentoo breeds in huge colonies.

The Rockhopper
It can climb steep rocks by hopping.

The Chinstrap
This penguin defends its young fiercely.

The Macaroni
Only the larger one of two eggs laid, hatches.

The King
This big penguin eats fish, squid and krill.

BIRDS

Some birds live at the poles all year round. Others nest and breed at the poles in their millions in the spring and summer when there is plenty of food. The most famous Antarctic birds are penguins. But petrels, skuas and albatrosses also nest on islands along the Antarctic coast.

Arctic tern
Each year the Arctic tern flies from the Arctic to Australia and back again, a distance of more than 40,000 kilometres. This is the longest journey made by any animal in the world.

Kittiwake
Building its nest on cliffs keeps the kittiwake safe from foxes and bears.

Puffin
A puffin can hold as many as fifty herrings at the same time in its colourful beak.

Little auk
This is one of fourteen species of auk, and lives on the Arctic cliffs.

In winter, some birds survive by eating roots and berries found under the snow, or small mammals and insects.

○ **Wandering albatross**
Soaring effortlessly over southern seas on its long, narrow wings, the albatross nests on islands along the Antarctic coast.

○ **Gannet**
The gannet catches fish by diving into the sea at speed, its wings neatly folded.

○ **Guillemot**
The guillemot breeds in the summer when there are plenty of fish to feed on.

○ **Snowy owl**
Unlike most owls, the snowy owl hunts during the day rather than at night.

LIFE BELOW THE ICE

There is an amazing, unseen world under the polar ice, where hundreds of different kinds of fish, shellfish and tiny creatures live. Tiny plants grow on the undersides of the ice and are eaten by small creatures such as krill. These, in turn, are eaten by larger animals such as fish and whales.

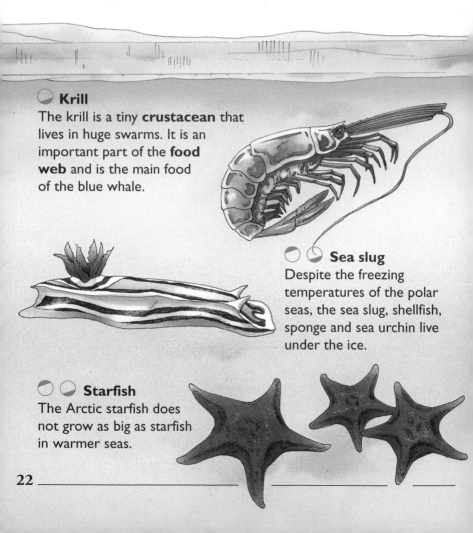

Krill
The krill is a tiny **crustacean** that lives in huge swarms. It is an important part of the **food web** and is the main food of the blue whale.

Sea slug
Despite the freezing temperatures of the polar seas, the sea slug, shellfish, sponge and sea urchin live under the ice.

Starfish
The Arctic starfish does not grow as big as starfish in warmer seas.

Only a few very hardy plants can grow round the South Pole. Crusty **lichens** and tiny plants called **algae** turn patches of the ice pinky-red.
A pink pigment helps to protect the algae from the Sun's harsh glare.

● Antarctic ice fish

Many polar fish, such as the Antarctic ice fish, have a kind of antifreeze in their blood to stop them from freezing solid.

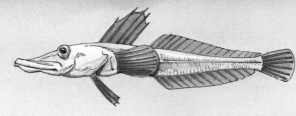

● ● Jellyfish

Some jellyfish have poisonous tentacles that they use to kill small fish.

● Cod

Found in the warmer Arctic waters, the cod is caught by people, for food.

EXPLORING THE POLES

Polar explorers face many problems. They must take the right clothes and supplies for the harsh conditions, and cope with hazards such as shifting ice and hungry polar bears. The most successful explorers are those who copy the ways Arctic people survive.

Robert Peary
The American explorer Robert Peary was probably the first person to reach the North Pole. He got there in 1909. Some people claim, however, that another American, Frederick Cook, beat Peary to it.

Roald Amundsen
Amundsen was the first person ever to reach the South Pole. With his party of four Norwegian explorers and a pack of fifty two dogs to pull sledges, he set out in October 1911. The party arrived at the Pole two months later, on 14 December 1911, almost a century after the continent of Antarctica was first discovered.

HUSKIES

Using husky dogs made Amundsen's journey much easier. Scott's men used up a lot of energy by pulling their own sledges.

Robert Scott

Robert Scott led the British expedition to the Antarctic. The team arrived at the South Pole on 17 January 1912, just thirty four days after Amundsen. On their way back to base camp, Scott and his entire team died. Scott wrote a diary that was found later.

Ranulph Fiennes

In 1993, two British explorers, Ranulph Fiennes and Michael Stroud, walked farther across Antarctica than anyone else had ever been. But, even with the help of hi-tech clothing and equipment, this two-man team suffered from severe **frostbite** and starvation.

PEOPLE OF THE POLES

The local Arctic people, called the Inuit, have lived near the North Pole for thousands of years and are experts at Arctic survival. They used to wander from place to place, hunting seals and polar bears. Today, many Inuit live in small towns.

Inuit lifestyle

The Inuit hunted seals as a source of food. They also used the seal skins for making clothes and tents, and the seal blubber for oil to burn in lamps.

The Inuit travelled by husky sledge and **kayak**. Igloos, built of blocks of ice, were used for shelter on hunting trips – igloos are surprisingly warm and cosy.

Some Inuit remain **nomadic** and continue their traditional ways, living from the land and sea.

Many Inuit live in settlements and use modern **skidoos** for transport.

Education in schools for Inuit children is now an important part of daily life.

Warm clothes, often made from animal skins, protect the Inuit against the cold.

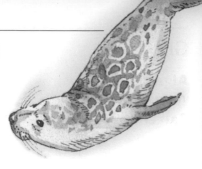

AMAZING POLAR FACTS

- **Penguins** Penguins can dive to depths of 265 metres. They may stay underwater without coming up to breathe for as long as eighteen minutes.

- **Narwhals** The long, twisted tusk of narwhals was once thought to be the horn of a unicorn. Only male narwhals have a tusk. This grows out of their lips and can reach a length of nearly three metres.

- **Killer whales** Killer whales can break through ice sheets which are a metre thick. They do this to throw seals resting on top of the ice sheet, into the sea. The whales can then catch the seals more easily in water. A killer whale may eat as many as twenty four seals in one meal.

- **Blue whales** Baby blue whales are the fastest growing creatures on Earth. They grow in weight from less than a milligram to twenty six tonnes in under two years. The calls of adult blue whales can be heard by other whales, from one end of an ocean to the other. These calls are the loudest sound made by any living animal.

- **Polar bears** Polar bears have no fear of people. They will hunt us if they are hungry. This makes polar bears the most dangerous mammals on the planet.

- **Icebergs** The largest iceberg ever recorded had an area of 31,000 square kilometres, making it bigger than the country of Belgium.

- **Arctic terns** An Arctic tern had a ring fitted to its leg when it was a chick in July 1955. The bird was then found less than a year later in Australia. It would have flown a distance of 22,530 kilometres to reach this continent.

GLOSSARY

Algae Tiny plants that grow in water or on wet land.

Baleen plates Sieve-like plates in a seal or whale's mouth. These plates allow it to take food out of the water.

Blowhole A small hole in the top of a whale's head that the whale breathes through.

Breathing hole A hole that a seal makes in the ice so that it can breathe.

Colony A large collection of birds or animals that lives in one area.

Crustacean An animal that is covered in a hard, protective shell.

Food web A term that describes the food cycle between plants and animals. For example, insects eat plants, birds eat insects, foxes eat birds, and when the fox dies, its body decomposes and fertilizes the plants.

Frostbite Freezing of parts of the body, often fingers and toes. This happens if a person is in a cold climate for too long, without suitable clothes.

Kayak A type of canoe where a person sits enclosed in the boat.

Krill A tiny creature that is covered in a hard shell and which lives in huge numbers.

Lichen A small plant that grows clinging to rocks and stones.

Mammal An animal that breathes air and can regulate its temperature.

Nomadic A way of life where people move around a large area with their homes and never settle in one place for longer than a few months.

North Pole The North Pole is an imaginary point that lies on the sea floor and not on the surface of the ice. It marks the northernmost point of the Earth's axis.

Skidoo A motorised sledge that can travel across the snow and ice at high speeds.

South Pole The South Pole is an imaginary point, marking the southern point of the Earth's axis.

Tundra An area of land in the Arctic that is frozen in winter but thaws on the surface during summer.

Tusk A long tooth of an animal that has grown outside the mouth.

INDEX *(Entries in **bold** refer to an illustration)*

A _pages_

Adelie penguin 19
albatross 20, 21
algae 23
Amundsen, Roald 24
Antarctic 6, 7, 12, 14, 20, 21, 23, 25
Antarctica 5, 7, 9, 24, 25
Antarctic Circle 5, 7
Antarctic ice fish 23
Arctic 6, 7, 8, 12, 14,16, 18, 20, 23, 24, 26
Arctic circle 5, 6
Arctic fox 10
Arctic Ocean 5, 17
Arctic tern 20, 28

B

beluga whale 15
bergy bit 9
bird 11, 20-21
blubber 11, 26
blue whale 14, 22, 28

C

chinstrap penguin 19
cod 23
Cook, Frederick 24
crabeater seal 13
crevasse 9

E

emperor penguin 18
Equator 5

F _pages_

Fiennes, Ranulph 25
fish 12, 19, 21, 22, 23

G

gannet 21
gentoo penguin 19
glacier 8, 9
growler 8
guillemot 21

H

harp seal 12
hooded seal 12
husky dog 24, 25

I

iceberg 8, 9, 28
ice floe 15, 16
ice sheet 8, 9
igloo 26
Inuit 26-27

J

jellyfish 23

K

killer whale 15, 28
king penguin 19
kittiwake 20
krill 13, 14, 19, 22

L

leopard seal 13
lichen 23
little auk 20